RIVERS
OF THE WORLD

THE VOLGA RIVER

Joanne Mattern

Mitchell Lane
PUBLISHERS

P.O. Box 196
Hockessin, Delaware 19707

RIVERS
OF THE WORLD

The Amazon River

The Nile River

The Ganges River

The Mississippi River

The Rhine River

The Tigris (Euphrates) River

The Yangtze River

The Volga River

PUBLISHER'S NOTE: The facts on which the story in this book is based have been thoroughly researched. Documentation of such research can be found on page 45. While every possible effort has been made to ensure accuracy, the publisher will not assume liability for damages caused by inaccuracies in the data, and makes no warranty on the accuracy of the information contained herein.

Printing   1   2   3   4   5   6   7   8   9

Library of Congress
Cataloging-in-Publication Data
Mattern, Joanne, 1963-
The Volga river / by Joanne Mattern.
     p. cm.—(Rivers of the world)
 Includes bibliographical references and index.
 ISBN 978-1-61228-312-8 (library bound)
1. Volga River Region (Russia)—Juvenile
literature. I. Title.
 DK511.V65M358 2012
 947'.4—dc23
                                          2012009470
eBook ISBN: 9781612283739

PLB

CONTENTS

Chapter One
  Battle on the River 5
  What's in a Name? 11
Chapter Two
  The Path of the Volga 13
  The Swaying Bridge 17
Chapter Three
  History of the Volga 19
  Fast Facts 23
  "The Volga Boatman" 27
Chapter Four
  Life Along the Volga 29
  Beautiful Astrakhansky Zapovednik 35
Chapter Five
  A Changing River 37
  Volga Day 43
Chapter Notes 44
Works Consulted 44
Further Reading 45
  Books 45
  On the Internet 45
Glossary 46
Index 47

The Volga River at sunset

CHAPTER 1

Battle on the River

World War II changed the face of the world. One of the nations that suffered the most during this terrible conflict was the Soviet Union, which consisted of Russia and 14 other republics. By the middle of 1942, the invading German army had killed or captured more than six million Soviet soldiers and occupied a large part of its land and resources.[1] The worst was yet to come. In the summer of 1942, Germany's Nazi leader, Adolf Hitler, set his sights on the southwestern part of the Soviet Union. His decision would lead to one of the most brutal and important battles of World War II. That battle was fought on the shores of the Volga River, in the city of Stalingrad.

Hitler had three main objectives in attacking Stalingrad. Stalingrad was a major industrial and transportation center, with many factories dedicated to producing weapons and other materials for the war effort. If the German army could destroy these factories, it would seriously hurt the Soviet Union's ability to arm its soldiers. Hitler also wanted to move

Soviet Marines arrive on the banks of the Volga River to prepare for battle against the German army.

closer to the oil-rich fields around the Caspian Sea. His third objective was to control the Volga River, the main waterway of the European portion of the Soviet Union. If Hitler controlled the Volga, he could prevent supplies such as weapons, fuel, and food from reaching Soviet troops. This would be a major step in defeating the Soviet army.

The Battle of Stalingrad started in July, 1942. The first attacks came by air. The German air force, or Luftwaffe, pounded Stalingrad with bombs that destroyed most of the city. Then the German army surged forward. Germany had help from its allies, as troops from Italy, Romania, and Hungary marched with the Germans, moving along the sides, or flanks, of the mighty German army.

The leader of the Soviet Union, Joseph Stalin, was very worried about the German advance. He issued an order commanding Soviet citizens to defend "every granule of Soviet soil to the last drop of blood."[2] The Soviets fought hard to defend their land and their city, but the German advance was too much. On August 23, advance elements of the German forces reached the Volga River just north of Stalingrad. The Germans took control of a strip of land along the river and sank any Soviet ship that came down the river. They even sank ferries carrying people trying to escape the city.

Stalingrad would not go down without a fight. Stalin sent two of his best generals to Stalingrad, as well as thousands of soldiers to defend the city. One Soviet division rushed across the Volga just in time to defeat a German attack in the center of the city. The Russians won that effort, but sadly, almost every Russian soldier in the division was killed or wounded in the fighting.

By fall, the Germans controlled the center of Stalingrad all the way to the Volga on the eastern side of the city. However, the Soviets refused to give up. The Soviet army pushed close to the German lines. This movement resulted in vicious hand-to-hand fighting through the streets of Stalingrad. For weeks, battles raged inside bombed-out shells of buildings. Soldiers fought in destroyed factories, houses, and apartment buildings. There were scenes where Soviet soldiers on one floor of a building fought through the floorboards to reach German soldiers on the floor below. Battles even raged underground in the miles of sewer and water tunnels that stretched under the city. "Stalingrad is no longer a town…it is an enormous cloud of burning, blinding smoke,"[3] said one German officer.

Despite the horrors, Hitler and Stalin refused to give up. Both leaders sent more troops to Stalingrad. The Soviets also came up with a clever plan. They secretly gathered troops west and south of Stalingrad. More than a million soldiers massed along the Volga and circled toward the Germans. By the time the Germans realized what was happening, it was too late. The Soviets attacked the flanks of the enemy forces, where the Italian, Romanian, and Hungarian armies were. These armies were poorly supplied and fell quickly. Just four days later,

the Soviets completely surrounded the German army in the center of Stalingrad. The Germans were trapped, but they refused to give up.

Then winter set in, and things got even worse for the troops on both sides. Because neither army could safely cross the Volga, food and other supplies could not be delivered. Many soldiers starved to death. Still more froze to death in the brutal Russian winter. The weather was so cold that everything froze solid—the ground, the river, even the engines of the airplanes. Thousands more died of disease from the brutal conditions. The Soviets were more accustomed to the freezing weather, which saw day after day of temperatures that plunged well below zero. Their soldiers had warmer uniforms, which helped them withstand the cold better than the Germans. However, as the weeks passed, it became harder and harder to bring in supplies, and soon the Soviets were no better off than the trapped Germans. Still, neither side would give up.

Soviet soldiers struggle to adapt to the harsh conditions as they attack German positions with a 45-millimeter cannon.

The German commander in Stalingrad was General Friedrich von Paulus. On January 24, 1942, von Paulus sent a message to Hitler saying, "Further defense senseless. Collapse inevitable. Army requests immediate permission to surrender in order to save lives."[4] Hitler refused von Paulus's desperate plea. Instead, Hitler promoted von Paulus to field marshal on January 30. He also reminded von Paulus that no field marshal had ever been captured alive, hinting that it would be humiliating if von Paulus was the first to do so. By that point, von Paulus didn't care. He surrendered the next day. Fighting continued in the city for a few more days, but the Battle of Stalingrad finally ended on February 2, 1943, after 200 long, deadly days.

General Friedrich von Paulus

The Battle of Stalingrad was one of the most important battles of the entire war. It was a major victory and turning point for the Soviet Union and marked the end of the German advance in that part of the world. The battle was also a huge blow to German morale. For the first time, Germans realized that they were not invincible and that they could lose major battles. The surviving Soviet soldiers who fought in the battle were considered heroes and were given the honor of leading the Soviet army into Berlin near the end of the war in 1945. Stalingrad itself was named a Hero City in 1945 and King George VI of Great Britain gifted the city with the jeweled Sword of Stalingrad to honor its bravery. Because the city had been completely destroyed in the battle, it was rebuilt after the war ended in 1945.

Russian T-34 tanks in the central area of Stalingrad on the day of the surrender of German forces on January 31, 1943.

Despite all these honors, the cost of Stalingrad in human lives was tremendous. More than a million Soviet soldiers and civilians were killed, wounded, or missing. Over 750,000 German, Romanian, Italian, and Hungarian soldiers were killed or wounded. In addition, more than 100,000 German soldiers were taken prisoner. Only 5,000 returned home at the end of the war.[5]

The Soviets were able to hold onto Stalingrad and eventually win the war. All this drama and devastation took place on the banks of one of Russia's most important and best-loved rivers, the Volga. Over the course of history, this river has seen many changes and major events.

What's in a Name?

Volgograd Station

Stalingrad is one of Russia's most famous cities, yet you won't find it on any modern maps. That's because the city's name has changed several times over the centuries. Stalingrad was not even the city's original name. In 1589, a settlement along the Volga was named Tsaritsyn, which means "yellow water." In 1925, Joseph Stalin renamed the city after himself in honor of his victory over opposing forces during the Russian Civil War that began in 1917. The city was called Stalingrad until 1961. At that time, the Soviet government was trying to get rid of references to Stalin, a dictator who was no longer admired. So Stalingrad became Volgograd in reference to its location on the Volga River. The suffix "-grad" means "city" in Russian, so the name translates to "Volga city." Although Volgograd has been the city's name for more than 50 years, many people want to change the name back to Stalingrad because of the enormous historical significance of that name in the battle during World War II.

Stalingrad is not the only Russian city whose name has changed over the years. Another major city, Saint Petersburg, was known as Petrograd between 1914 and 1924, and Leningrad between 1924 and 1991. In 1991, it went back to its original name.

Even the name of the country has changed. During the Communist rule between 1922 and 1991, Russia was called the Soviet Union. After the fall of Communism, the country's name went back to Russia.

Through all of these changes, at least the name of the Volga River has stayed the same!

A view of the Volga river in Nizhniy Novgorod, Russia

CHAPTER 2

The Path of the Volga

Russia is such a huge country that it spans two continents. The western part of Russia is in Europe, while the eastern part lies in Asia. A country this big has many important rivers, and the Volga is the most important.

The Volga is the longest river in Europe. It measures 2,294 miles (3,692 kilometers) in length. More water flows through the Volga than any other European river. The river and its tributaries drain an area of about 550,288 square miles (1,410,994 square kilometers), which is about forty percent of European Russia.[1]

The Volga begins near the tiny village of Volgoverkhovye in the Valdai Hills. A small chapel has been built at this site. The Valdai Hills are not very high, and the Volga is only 740 feet (225 meters) above sea level at its starting point.

The Volga doesn't run in a straight line. From the Valdai Hills, the Volga heads east. It passes Lake Sterzh, and the cities of Tver, Dubna, Rybinsk,

Yaroslavl, Nizhny Novgorod, and Kazan. At Kazan, the river turns south, flowing past Ulyanovsk, Tolyatti, Samara, Saratov, and Volgograd. At Volgograd, the river takes another twist, turning sharply to the east. From there the river flows south to the city of Astrakhan, on the northern edge of the Caspian Sea.

The Volga River ends its journey where it empties into the Caspian Sea. At this point, the elevation of the Volga is 92 feet (28 meters) below sea level. Unlike some rivers, which start high in the mountains and drop sharply over their course, the Volga's elevation changes by less than a thousand feet. Because the river runs through such relatively flat terrain, its water flows more slowly compared to most other rivers.

The Caspian Sea is the largest body of inland water in the world. One of the most important features of the Volga River is at its end, where a huge delta has formed as it drains into the Caspian. This delta is covered with the soil and nutrients that the Volga has carried for more than two thousand miles. The shallow delta contains large areas of sand and mud deposited there by the river. These sandy and muddy areas provide a rich environment for plants and animals.

Many other rivers, or tributaries, branch off from the Volga. The most important are the Kama River and the Oka River. The Kama River branches to the east, while the Oka River branches to the west. Other tributaries include the Vetluga and the Sura Rivers. These rivers all form what is called the Volga river system. This system drains most of western Russia and includes about five hundred channels and smaller rivers. The Volga river system creates the largest estuary in Europe.

Many cities developed along the Volga, and the river became an important source of transportation for both people and goods. A number of bridges cross the river. The first, near the Volga's source near Volgoverkhovye, is only nine feet (3 meters) long. As the river gets wider, the cities along its banks get bigger, and so do their bridges. The longest is the Saratov Bridge. It crosses the Volga at the city of Saratov, about 206 miles (331 kilometers) upstream from Volgograd. This bridge was opened in 1965 and is 9,198 feet (2,804 meters) long. When it was

The Saratov Bridge connects the city of Saratov on the west bank of the Volga with the city of Engels on the east bank. Residents had long wanted a bridge to connect both sides of the river, but a lack of technical resources meant it took years for the bridge to actually be built.

built, the Saratov was the longest bridge in the Soviet Union as well as in Europe, although it doesn't hold either of those distinctions today.

Over the years, the Russian government has taken advantage of the Volga and used it to connect cities to each other. As far back as the early 1700s, Tsar Peter the Great began building canals. The most ambitious was begun in 1709 and called the Mariinsk system. This canal connected the Rybinsk Reservoir at the northern part of the Volga with Saint Petersburg. These canals made it much easier to transport goods from the southern part of the country to the north and back again. During the 1930s and again in the 1960s, the Mariinsk system was enlarged and improved. Today, the canal and river system is called the Volga-Baltic Waterway. The waterway covers about 685 miles (1,100 kilometers) and provides an important route for transporting goods.

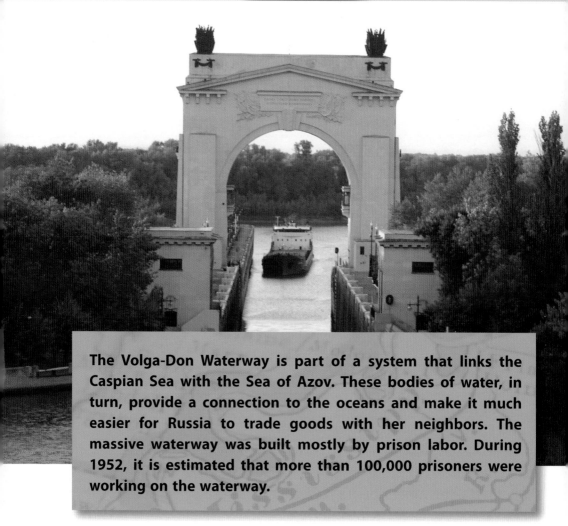

The Volga-Don Waterway is part of a system that links the Caspian Sea with the Sea of Azov. These bodies of water, in turn, provide a connection to the oceans and make it much easier for Russia to trade goods with her neighbors. The massive waterway was built mostly by prison labor. During 1952, it is estimated that more than 100,000 prisoners were working on the waterway.

Peter the Great also tried to connect the Volga with the Don, a river that flows from south of Moscow to the Sea of Azov, an inlet of the Black Sea. Peter was not able to complete the project. More than 200 years later, during the 1940s, work began again on a canal to connect the two rivers. Finally, in 1952, the Volga-Don Canal was completed. The canal uses a series of locks to raise and lower ships carrying coal, minerals, building materials, and grain along the passage between the Don and the Volga. By connecting the two major rivers, Russia greatly improved its transportation system and took full advantage of the Volga's power.

The Swaying Bridge

Volgograd Bridge

One of the newest bridges over the Volga is also one of the most troublesome. In 2009, after 13 years of construction, the Volgograd Bridge finally opened to traffic. This bridge and its access roads are almost four and a half miles (7.1 kilometers) long. Surprisingly, this was the first bridge built over the Volga at Volgograd. Before the bridge was built, the only way to drive over the river was to take a road over the Volga Hydroelectric Station dam. Authorities in Volgograd plan to build more bridges over the Volga in the next few years.

The bridge was only open for seven months when trouble struck. On May 20, 2010, officials had to close the bridge because it was swaying and moving up and down in a strong wind. The Voice of Russia radio network reported that the shaking was so severe that cars were sent into the air and drove into oncoming traffic. Many drivers thought they were experiencing an earthquake.[2] No one was allowed to drive over the bridge until it was inspected for safety. Finally, on May 25, the bridge was reopened to traffic even as experts continued to study its safety. Video of the shaking bridge can still be seen on the Internet.

Ovid among the Scythians, 1862, by Eugène Delacroix, depicts an outcast poet of Rome helped by the Scythian people along the river.

CHAPTER 3

History of the Volga

The Volga River is a beloved part of Russian history and culture. Russians often call the river "Mother Volga" and there are many songs, paintings, and stories celebrating the Volga and the people who live on or near its waters. This river and the area around it have been an important part of Russia's history and culture for more than a thousand years.

The western part of Russia was first settled by people known as Scythians. Scythians were a nomadic people originally from what is now the country of Iran. They migrated from Central Asia to southern Russia during the eighth and seventh centuries BCE. They ruled the area until about the second century AD, when they were defeated and chased out of the area by other Asian tribes, including the Huns and the Turks. At about the same time, the Volga was first mentioned in Ptolemy's reference book *Geography*. Ptolemy, an ancient Roman mathematician, astronomer, and geographer, called the river Rha, which was the Scythian word for "river."

By the ninth century AD, the Volga had become an important waterway and transportation route for

This painting, *Battle Between the Scythians and the Slavs,* was painted by famous Russian artist Viktor Vasnetsov in 1881. Vasnetsov lived between 1848-1926 and often used historical and mythological subjects in his work.

many tribes traveling between Asia and Europe. The most powerful of these tribes were the Slavs. The Slavs were described as tall, blond, handsome, and strong. They were brave fighting men who fought off raids from the Vikings in Scandinavia as well as nomadic tribes throughout Europe. In time, a group called the East Slavs migrated into the forests and steppes of what is now eastern Russia. Today's ethnic Russians are descended from the East Slavs, and the Slavic language is the ancestor of the modern Russian language.

The Slavs were powerful warriors, but during peacetime they were farmers. They settled along the banks of the Volga and across the steppes, where they found the grasslands to be a fertile growing place. The Slavs raised grasses and grains such as rye, barley, and millet. They also hunted, fished, and traded with each other for goods. In time, the Slavic empire grew into a state called Kievan Rus.

The eastern side of the Volga was settled by another ethnic group, the Mongols. By the thirteenth century, the Mongols were powerful enough to threaten Kievan Rus. By the end of the 1250s, the Mongols, now called the Tatar Khans after their leader, Batu Khan, had defeated Kievan Rus. The victors founded a state called the Golden Horde in the lower part of the Volga. The Tatars remained in power until 1480, when Tsar Ivan III began unifying the different tribes in Russia to create one country.

Russia may have been unified, but all the fighting left the country in sad shape and far behind Western Europe in its development, industry, and culture. In 1689, Tsar Peter I came to the throne. Peter was only seventeen years old, but he was such a powerful and influential ruler that he became known as Peter the Great. Over his nearly 36-year rule, Peter built arms and weapons factories, textile industries, and other businesses. He improved Russia's transportation system so the country could trade both within its borders and with other countries. One of Peter's greatest transportation projects was a series of canals that linked the Volga River and the Neva River. These canals made it much easier to transport goods between northern and southern Russia.

Russia continued to develop and prosper, and so did the Volga River. Many people settled along its banks and in the fertile farmlands of the nearby steppes. Soon the river was dotted with major cities, including Kazan, Astrakhan, and Tsaritsyn (later known as Stalingrad and then Volgograd). Many religious shrines and monasteries were also built along the banks of the river.

Catherine II, known as Catherine the Great, was the empress of Russia from 1762 to 1796. She was German by birth and in 1763 she invited German families to settle in Russia after she came to power. Many Germans accepted her invitation because of harsh conditions at home caused by war and other difficulties. By contrast, Catherine offered what sounded like paradise in Russia: "readily available land for purchase, exemption from military service, freedom from most taxation, self administration, religious freedom and loans to aid their initial

Catherine the Great ruled Russia longer than any other female leader. She had many accomplishments, including greatly expanding the size of the Russian empire, improving the country's foreign policy, and Westernizing the country to make it more competitive with other European nations.

settlements."[1] The German government put a stop to this emigration in 1767, but by that time an estimated 25,000 to 30,000 Germans had moved to Russia.[2] In time, a large German community settled near the city of Saratov on the Volga River. Most of the emigrants were young families, including many couples who had just married. By the late 1800s, there were 192 German villages and towns clustered along the Volga. These settlers became known as the Volga Germans.

Life became more difficult for the Germans during the 1870s. The government wanted the Germans to become more Russian and abandon their traditions. Young German men were also forced to join the Russian army. As opportunities in Russia declined, many Volga Germans emigrated to the United States to start a new life.

FAST FACTS

- Origin of name: From the Slavic word "Volga," which means "wetness"

- Countries: Russia

- Cities: Astrakhan, Volgograd, Saratov, Samara, Kazan, Ulyanovsk, Nizhny Novgorod, Yaroslavl, Tver

- Primary source: in the Valdai Hills near Tver Oblast

- Elevations: 740 feet (225 meters) in the Valdai Hills; 92 feet (28 meters) below sea level at the mouth in the Caspian Sea

- Coordinates: 45°50'30"N, 47°58'17"E

- Mouth: the Caspian Sea

- Length: 2,294 miles (3,692 kilometers)

- Width: varies, up to several miles wide

In 1917, Russia's tsar was overthrown by a Communist government. Five years later, Russia and several neighboring countries became one nation, called the Soviet Union or USSR. A small area of the Volga region was renamed the Volga German Autonomous Soviet Socialist Republic and was used to house many of the remaining Volga Germans. Other Germans moved out of the area. During World War II, when Germany was the enemy, the Volga German ASSR was disbanded and the home of the Volga Germans disappeared.

In the Soviet Union, all aspects of life were controlled by the government. This control extended to factories and transportation. Many cities were built solely to provide factories and workers for industrial production. These cities were usually located near rivers and other bodies of water to provide easy access to natural resources and transportation. The Volga was no exception. Today the Volga's banks are lined with petroleum and natural gas refineries, as well as other heavy industries.

In addition to factories, the Soviets also built a series of dams along the Volga. These dams changed the flow of the river and made it more

Lake Rybinsk may look like an ocean, but it is really a large reservoir.

Cargo ships like these are free to travel along Russian waters.

suitable for transportation. They also created reservoirs so the Volga's water could be used to irrigate crops and provide drinking water for people. Soviet-built reservoirs include the Rybinsk, which was the largest artificial lake in the world at the time it was built, the Ivankovo, the Gorky, and the Kubyshev, which today is the largest reservoir in Europe. These dams allowed large cargo ships carrying grain, oil, and other goods to travel up and down the Volga and link with other parts of Russia through several systems of canals. During the Soviet era, only Soviet ships were allowed on the Volga. However, after the Soviet Union collapsed in 1991, Russia began allowing ships from other nations, particularly in Europe, to travel on the river as well.

Russia is such a huge country that it has always been hard for the government to control all the many regions and ethnic groups in the nation. Part of the problem is that while ethnic Russians make up more than half of the population, the remainder is composed of minority groups, including Turks, Chechens, Armenians, Germans, Gypsies, and many more. There are also a variety of different religious groups, including Jews, Christians, and Muslims. After the breakup of the Soviet

A group from the United Nations visits the Itelmans, a small ethnic group who are the original inhabitants of the Kamchatka Peninsula in the easternmost portion of Russia. Today the population of full-blooded Itelmans is only about 1500.

Union in 1991, there was a lot of unrest as minority groups struggled to form their own governments.

One of the areas with the most unrest was along the Volga. The area has a large population of Tatars, who declared themselves to be the ethnic republic of Tatarstan. The Tatars are one of the largest minority ethnic groups in Russia and live in an area rich in railroads, oil pipelines, and major industries, so it was vital to the Russian government to stay in control of this region. In 1995, Tatarstan declared itself a republic that is part of the Russian Federation, but in 2002, the constitution was changed and Tatarstan officials declared the area was part of Russia. The region escaped the bloodshed and warfare that plagued other areas of Russia where ethnic and religious groups demanded sovereignty.

"The Volga Boatman"

"The Volga Boatman" is one of Russia's most popular traditional
folk songs. The song is a shanty, or sea-chant, a rhythmic tune
sung by the boatmen who hauled barges up and down the Volga
during the days of the tsars. The song was inspired by the famous
1872 painting by Ilya Yefimovich Repin, called *Burlaks [Boatmen]
on the Volga*, which showed the hardships of life under the tsars.

Its lyrics are as follows:
Yo, heave ho! Yo, heave ho!
Once more, once again, still once more.
Now we fell the stout birch tree,
Now we pull hard: one, two, three.
Ay-da, da, ay-da!
Ay-da, da, ay-da!
Now we fell the stout birch tree.
Yo, heave ho!
Hey, hey, let's heave a-long the way,
To the sun we sing our song.
Yo, heave ho! Yo, heave ho!
Once more, once again, still once more.
As the barges float along,
To the sun we sing our song.
Ay-da, da, ay-da!
Ay-da, da, ay-da!
To the sun we sing our song.
Hey, hey, let's heave a-long the way,
To the sun we sing our song.
Yo, heave ho! Yo, heave ho!
Once more, once again, still once more.
Volga, Volga our pride,
Mighty stream so deep and wide.
Ay-da, da, ay-da!
Ay-da, da, ay-da!
Mighty stream so deep and wide.
Volga, Volga you're our pride.
Yo, heave ho! Yo, heave ho!
Once more, once again, still once more.[3]

Taiga forests filled with evergreen trees stretch along the Volga and many other rivers in Russia.

CHAPTER 4

Life Along the Volga

The land along the Volga is very different from start to finish. The river begins in the forests and moves through grassy fields and plains.

The Volga River starts in an area of thick forests called taiga. Taiga forests include evergreen trees such as pines, spruces, and firs. These trees have needles rather than leaves and keep their needles all year long. Many animals live in these thick forests, including elk, reindeer, wolves, brown bears, beavers, lynx, foxes, and rabbits.

As the river moves south, it passes through deciduous forests. These forests are made up mostly of birch trees but also include aspens, lindens, cedars, oaks, limes, elms, and maples. Deciduous trees lose their leaves every fall and grow new ones during the spring. Mosses and ferns also grow in these forests. These plants thrive in the damp, cool conditions. Deer, lynx, wolves, foxes, and many smaller mammals live in these forests.

As the Volga continues to travel south, the landscape changes. The forests are replaced by a landform called steppes. Steppes are grasslands with small shrubs and bushes but no tall trees. The steppes of the Volga are very fertile and used for growing wheat and other cereal crops.

The ground becomes drier as the Volga gets closer to the Caspian Sea. There is even a small area of desert here, where few plants grow. This desert occurs because there are few streams branching off from the Volga to irrigate the ground, making it dry and dusty.

At the end of the river's course, an amazing thing happens. The river opens into the beautiful Volga River delta. The delta is created as the Volga splits into a fan of more than 250 channels that flow through the landscape. The Volga River delta is one of the largest deltas in the world.

The delta supports a variety of plant life. Willow trees are common along the banks of the river, dangling their long branches into the water. In the summer, the delta is covered by hundreds of pink and white lotus flowers that grow on the surface of the water. Lotus flowers open and bloom for only three days. These beautiful flowers have tall blue-gray leaves that stand above the water. Lotus flowers can be up to 30 inches wide and grow up to six feet high, creating a colorful carpet on the water. Other water plants in the delta include pondweeds, milfoil, and water lilies.

The Volga River delta also supports a rich variety of animal life. More than 250 types of birds are found there. The delta is one of the world's most important nesting grounds for water birds. It is the only place in Russia where you can find flamingos and pelicans. Other

A sandpiper runs along the banks of the Volga River. These shorebirds are a common sight along the river's beaches as they look for food in the sand and shallow water.

common birds are eagles, swans, ducks, geese, egrets, cranes, cormorants, and kingfishers. More than 25,000 ducks have been seen on the water during the summer. Away from the water, many birds nest in the forests that grow along the river. These birds include wood pigeons, golden orioles, tree sparrows, warblers, and cuckoos.

Most of the birds on the river feed on the many different fish, amphibians, and snakes that live in and around the water. Frogs and toads are common here, as well as grass snakes, sand lizards, and rat snakes. There are also more than 60 different types of fish in the Volga River delta. The most common fish is the carp. These fish pull their bodies out of the water to lay eggs on the ground or in the shallow water. After the eggs hatch, the young fish swim into the deeper water. Pike, perch, bream, and goldfish are also found in the delta. These fish can be found in schools of hundreds or even thousands. The Volga is also an important migration route for herring, which travel from the Caspian Sea to the upper Volga where they lay their eggs.

The wild boar is the largest animal to live in the forests along the Volga. This wild pig eats many different foods, but most of its diet is made of plants such as roots, leaves, and grass.

The delta is also home to about 30 different species of mammals. The largest mammal in the area is the wild boar. Other delta mammals include foxes, raccoons, weasels, minks, beavers, muskrats, and mice.

After the Volga moves through the delta, it flows into the Caspian Sea. The Caspian Sea is one of the most important bodies of water in Russia. The "sea" is actually the world's largest lake, and covers more than 144,402 square miles (374,000 square kilometers). Many fish live in the Caspian Sea, but the largest and most important is the sturgeon.

Three species of sturgeon live in the Caspian Sea and sometimes swim up into the Volga River delta. These species are the Russian sturgeon, the stellate sturgeon, and the beluga sturgeon. The beluga is the largest species of sturgeon. This fish can live up to one hundred years. It grows up to thirty feet (nine meters) long and weighs up to 1,800 pounds (816 kilograms). More than 80 percent of the world's sturgeon live in the Caspian Sea.

**Sturgeon fish common
in Russian waters**

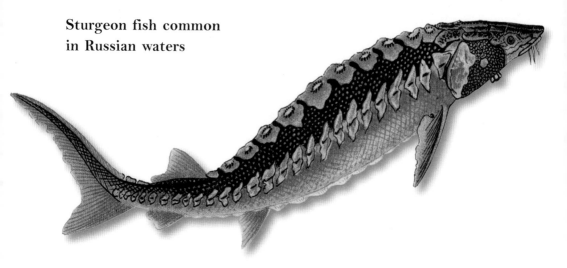

Sturgeon are valued because of their eggs. These eggs are sold as a food called caviar. Caviar is a popular everyday food in Russia and other parts of Eastern Europe, and it has become very popular in the United States and other parts of the world as well. Russia and the other countries that border the Caspian Sea have made a lot of money selling caviar, but this industry has severely damaged the sturgeon population. Today, scientists have said that "there are not enough sturgeons being left to reproduce and maintain their population. Once the sturgeons die out, the money from the caviar industry will disappear."[1]

The overfishing of sturgeon was not a problem before the breakup of the Soviet Union, because at that time only the Soviet Union and Iran fished in the Caspian Sea. Their governments had strict rules about how many sturgeon could be caught each year. After the breakup of the Soviet Union, however, new nations formed along the Caspian Sea and there was no longer as much oversight over how sturgeons were fished. In addition, many people poach, or fish illegally, further harming the sturgeon population. Sturgeons have been called the prehistoric fish because they have been on Earth for millions of years, but it will take stricter rules and government control to make sure that this important Volga fish survives in the 21st century.

Beautiful Astrakhansky Zapovednik

Astrakhansky Zapovednik

Russians are eager to preserve the wild beauty and variety of life in the delta. As far back as 1919, part of the delta was declared a conservation area and named Astrakhansky Zapovednik. It was the first wildlife preserve formed under Soviet rule. During the late 1970s and 1980s, the preserve gained national recognition for its preservation of many wild species of animals and plants. The World Wildlife Fund named the delta a Wetland of International Importance because it provides a habitat for millions of migrating birds. More than 250 species can be found in its 254 square miles (668 km²).

During the Soviet era, the government gave a lot of money to Astrakhansky Zapovednik. The preserve was the pride of the Soviet government and wildlife flourished there. Scientists studied animals and plants in the preserve and the government made sure strict conservation laws were enforced.

Unfortunately, since the fall of the Soviet Union in 1991, there hasn't been as much money available to the preserve. Poachers and hunters have been able to get into the preserve and destroy wildlife and plant life. Even tourists can damage the preserve by disturbing nesting sites and other wild areas. Pollution along the Volga River from industry has also damaged Astrakhansky Zapovednik and decreased the number of plants, fish, birds, and other animals that are able to survive there. Today, the area is still an important wildlife preserve but it is in danger.

Swimmers enjoy the Volga in Samara, Russia

CHAPTER 5

A Changing River

The Volga River has undergone many changes over the past few hundred years. It is definitely not the same river that the Slavs saw when they migrated east and settled along the great river's banks. Industrialization has had a major effect on the river and the areas around it.

In its natural state, the Volga was a slow-moving river flowing along a fairly narrow route from the northern forests, through the steppes, and finally emptying into the Caspian Sea. However, things changed as people began relying on the river for transportation, irrigation, and other necessities. The river was linked to other Russian waterways through a series of canals. These changes made it possible for larger ships to navigate the Volga, bringing more traffic to the once-peaceful waters.

During the 1920s, the new Soviet government began changing the Volga's course even more. The government built a series of dams and locks along the river. These changes not only improved

The Volga Hydropower Station is the largest hydroelectric power station in Europe. It was part of a huge effort initiated by Soviet leader Joseph Stalin to rebuild the nation after World War II. Work on the station began in 1950 and it went into service in 1961.

transportation, but they also allowed people to use the Volga's water as a source of energy, especially to create hydroelectric power. The largest of these dams were built near the cities of Rybinsk, Nizhny Novgorod, Samara, and Stalingrad (Volgograd). However, the many large reservoirs made the Volga's course more like a series of lakes than a flowing river. In a startling statistic, author Michael Kort points out that water that once took five days to flow from the northern city of Rybinsk to Volgograd, near the Caspian Sea, now takes 500 days to make the same journey.[1]

As years passed, the Soviets continued to stress economic development at any cost. Over the next few decades, people relied even more on the Volga's water as a source of power. Factories and

The gigantic The Motherland Calls statue in Volgograd towers 279 feet (85 meters) from the base to the tip of the sword. At its dedication in 1967, it was the largest piece of sculpture in the world. The 200 steps leading to the statue symbolize the 200 days of the Battle of Stalingrad.

electric plants continued to rise along the shores. Heavy industry came to the area with factories building trucks and processing chemicals. There are also large oil deposits under the land between the Volga and the Ural Mountains. The oil from these fields is processed at large petroleum plants built along the Volga's banks. All in all, there are more than two hundred major industrial complexes along the Volga.

While the Volga River does provide a source of energy for many different industries, those industries may be killing the river itself. Pollution from the factories and the ships that travel along the river has severely affected the Volga. Today it is one of Russia's most polluted rivers. The pollution in the Volga affects everything around it, from the farmlands that cover the steppes to the fish populations of the Volga and the Caspian Sea. The millions of tons of industrial waste flowing into the river have killed millions of fish and sickened those that have survived, devastating both the fish populations as well as the fishing industry.

Factories like these are endangering the waters and wildlife of the Volga River at an alarming rate.

Parts of the Volga River are so choked with algae that it is impossible for other plants and fish to survive.

Pollution doesn't always kill wildlife. Sometimes it encourages the growth of undesirable vegetation. All the pollution flowing into the river has caused algae to grow. Algae use up the oxygen in the water and can grow so thickly that other plants and animals cannot survive.

All the Volga's polluted waters flow into the Caspian Sea. The Caspian Sea is the world's leading source of caviar, but this industry is threatened because pollution is one of the factors that have harmed the population of sturgeon in the water. Oil wells around the Caspian Sea also pollute the water, killing both plant and animal life. The Volga is not alone in suffering environmental devastation as a consequence of the Soviet government's policies. As President Boris Yeltsin said in 1993, following the collapse of the Soviet Union, "We have inherited an ecological disaster."[2]

The condition of the Volga is grim, but fortunately many people are working to save the river and its ecosystem. In 2006, the international organization UNESCO partnered with Coca-Cola HBC Eurasia to begin a program called "Living Volga." This conservation effort "aims to foster

The Volga reflects a clear blue sky.

better awareness and valuation of biodiversity resources of Volga water and wetlands ecosystems and understanding of the principles of sustainable development amongst local authorities and communities."[3] In simpler language, its goal is to help people understand why the Volga's ecosystem is important and to teach authorities and residents how to keep the river healthy. The program is achieving these goals through public education and training programs, publicizing the program through newspapers and other media, and meeting with local authorities and industry leaders to educate them on the importance of preserving the river and its ecosystems.

More than 60 million people depend on the Volga River for water, energy, and transportation, and the river is an important part of almost half of Russia's industry and agricultural businesses. More importantly, the river is a vital and beloved part of Russia's history, heritage, and culture. It is necessary and important that the river and all its riches are saved for future generations.

Volga Day

River pollution

As part of its efforts to restore the Volga River, UNESCO's Living Volga program features an annual festival called Volga Day. Volga Day has been held on May 20 every year since 2008. Volga Day is celebrated in the cities of Astrakhan, Volgograd, Nizhny Novgorod, Samara, and Yaroslavl, as well as in the Republic of Tatarstan. The celebrations are organized by several organizations, including UNESCO's Moscow office, Coca-Cola HBC Eurasia, the United Nations Development Program, and several wildlife reserves including the great Astrakhansky Zapovednik.

Volga Day celebrations include river bank cleanups, presentations of the cultural traditions of the region, scientific discussions on the topics of sustainable development, photo and painting exhibitions, concerts, games, and other activities. Organizers hope that Volga Day will draw attention to the rich heritage of the Volga and encourage the general public, environmental groups, and local officials to work together to find solutions to preserve the area's rich heritage. Most of all, Volga Day honors and attracts attention for the great river, the "Mother Volga."

After the fourth annual event was held in 2011, UNESCO officials declared, "With every year it [Volga Day] becomes more and more popular among local population, administration, business, and mass media. The variety of events organized during the Volga Day involves everyone: from children to representatives of scientific and business communities."[4]

Chapter 1: Battle on the River

1. "The Battle of Stalingrad."
   http://www.2worldwar2.com/stalingrad.htm.
2. Ibid.
3. "The Battle of Stalingrad Facts."
   http://ww2-pictures.com/battle-of-stalingrad-facts.htm.
4. Ibid.
5. Geoffrey Roberts, "Victory on the Volga." *The Guardian,* February 27, 2003. http://www.
   guardian.co.uk/world/2003/feb/28/russia.comment

Chapter 2: The Path of the Volga

1. "Volga River." http://world-geography.org/rivers/712-volga-river.html
2. "Bridge's St. Vitus Dance." http://english.ruvr.ru/rtvideo/2010/05/21/video_8243260.html

Chapter 3: History of the Volga

1. Herb Femling, "Volga Germans." http://www.femling.com/gen/balzer/volga.htm
2. Ibid.
3. "Volga Boatman Lyrics and History."
   http://www.makingmusicfun.net/htm/f_mmf_music_library_songbook/volga-
   boatman-history-and-lyrics.htm

Chapter 4: Life Along the Volga

1. "Giant and Common Sturgeon."
   http://www.lochnessinvestigation.org/sturgeon.html

Chapter 5: A Changing River

1. Michael Kort, *Nations in Transition: Russia,* revised edition (New York: Facts on File,
   1998), p.170.
2. Mike Edwards, "A Broken Empire." *National Geographic,* March 1993, p.9.
3. "Living Volga Programme." UNESCO. http://www.unesco.org/new/en/moscow/about-
   this-office/single-view/news/living_volga_programme-1/
4. "Volga Day 2011."
   http://www.unesco.org/new/en/moscow/about-this-office/single-view/news/
   volga_day_2011/?cHash=bb604a4a69666b581184367ed7f2e64d

Works Consulted

"Astrakhansky Zapovednik." Wild Russia.
   http://www.wild-russia.org/bioregion3/astrakhan/3_astrakhan.htm
"The Battle of Stalingrad."
   http://www.2worldwar2.com/stalingrad.htm
"The Battle of Stalingrad Facts."
   http://ww2-pictures.com/battle-of-stalingrad-facts.htm
Edwards, Mike. "A Broken Empire," *National Geographic,* March 1993.
Femling, Herb. "Volga Germans."
   http://www.femling.com/gen/balzer/volga.htm

"Flora and Fauna." Facts About Russia.
http://www.visaexpress.net/russia/flora.htm

"Giant and Common Sturgeon." http://www.lochnessinvestigation.org/sturgeon.html

Kort, Michael. *Nations in Transition: Russia,* revised edition. New York: Facts on File, 1998.

"Living Volga Programme." UNESCO. http://www.unesco.org/new/en/moscow/about-this-office/single-view/news/living_volga_programme-1/

Roberts, Geoffrey. "Victory on the Volga." *The Guardian,* February 27, 2003.
http://www.guardian.co.uk/world/2003/feb/28/russia.comment

"Volga-Baltic Waterway." http://www.factmonster.com/ce6/world/A0851118.html

"Volga Boatman Lyrics and History." http://www.makingmusicfun.net/htm/f_mmf_music_library_songbook/volga-boatman-history-and-lyrics.htm

"Volga Day 2011." http://www.unesco.org/new/en/moscow/about-this-office/single-view/news/volga_day_2011/?cHash=bb604a4a69666b581184367ed7f2e64d.

"Volga Germans." http://www.femling.com/gen/balzer/volga.htm

"The Volga River." http://www.sheppardsoftware.com/Europeweb/factfile/Unique-facts-Europe4.htm

"Volga River." http://world-geography.org/rivers/712-volga-river.html

"The Volga River Basin Report." http://www.irtces.org/isi/isi_document/2010/ISI_Case_study_Volga.pdf

"Volga River Delta." http://wwf.panda.org/about_our_earth/ecoregions/volga_river_delta.cfm

Further Reading

Books

Adams, Simon. *Changing World: Russia.* New York: Franklin Watts, 2010.

Fein, Eric. *Impossible Victory: The Battle of Stalingrad.* Mankato, Minnesota: Capstone, 2008.

Marquez, Heron. *Russia in Pictures.* Minneapolis: Lerner, 2009.

Russell, Henry. *National Geographic Countries of the World: Russia.* Washington, D.C.: National Geographic Children's Books, 2008.

Streissguth, Thomas. *Russia.* Minneapolis: Lerner, 2009.

Websites

"How Stuff Works: The Volga River."
http://geography.howstuffworks.com/asia/the-volga-river.htm

"Living Volga Partnership Programme"
http://www.projectwet.org/pdfs/conference-2011/Marie-Prchalova-CS11.pdf

"Rivers of Life: River Profiles: The Volga." http://cgee.hamline.edu/rivers/Resources/river_profiles/Volga.html

"Volga River."
http://www.volgawriter.com/VW%20Volga%20River.htm

"Volga River Pictures."
http://web.bryant.edu/~langlois/ecology/funpics.html

algae (AL-jee)—small plants without roots or stems that grow in water

canals (kuh-NALZ)—channels that are dug across land to connect bodies of water

Communist (KOM-yoo-nuhst)—a type of government in which the state owns all property

conservation (kon-ser-VAY-shun)—the protection of wildlife and natural resources

deciduous (duh-SID-yoo-us)—trees that lose their leaves every fall and grow new leaves in the spring

delta (DEL-tuh)—a triangular area of land where a river deposits mud and sand as it enters the sea

emigration (eh-muh-GRAY-shuhn)—leaving one country to live and work in another country

estuaries (ESS-chew-air-eez)—tidal inlets of an ocean or sea

ethnic (ETH-nik)—having to do with a group of people who share the same national origin, culture, and language

fertile (FER-tuhl)—able to support life

hydroelectric (high-droh-uh-LEK-trik)—having to do with electricity produced by the power of running water

irrigate (EAR-uh-gate)—to provide water to crops by artificial means

locks (LOKS)—parts of a canal with gates at each end where the water level can be raised or lowered to allow boats to pass through

monasteries (MAW-nuhs-tair-eez)—buildings where religious men called monks live and work

nomadic (no-MAD-ik)—moving from place to place

petroleum (puh-TROH-lee-uhm)—having to do with oil or gasoline

poachers (POH-churz)—people who kill animals and sell their body parts

reservoirs (REH-zuh-vwarz)—lakes caused by the building of a dam

steppes (STEPS)—grasslands with small shrubs and bushes but no tall trees

taiga (TY-guh)—a forest made up of evergreen trees

tsar (ZAR)—an emperor or leader of Russia before the Communist revolution

Index

Astrakhan   14, 21, 43
Astrakhansky Zapovednik   35, 43
Battle of Stalingrad   5-10
Black Sea   16
Caspian Sea   6, 14, 32, 33, 37-38, 40-41
Catherine the Great   21
caviar   34, 41
deciduous forests   29
Don River   16
East Slavs   20
Germans   5, 6-9, 10, 21-22
Hitler, Adolf   5, 6, 7, 9
Hungary   6, 7, 10
hydroelectric power   38
Italy   6, 7, 10
Ivan III   21
Kievan Rus   20, 21
Kort, Michael   38
"Living Volga"   41-42
Mariinsk system   15
Mongols   21
Peter the Great   15, 16, 21
Romania   6, 7, 10
Rybinsk   13, 24, 38
Saratov   14, 22
Saratov Bridge   14-15
Scythians   19
Sea of Azov   16
Slavic language   20
Slavs   20, 37
Soviet Union   5-10, 11, 15, 23, 24-26, 34
Stalin, Joseph   6-7, 11
Stalingrad   5, 7-10, 11, 21
sturgeon   33-34, 41
Sword of Stalingrad   9

taiga forests   29
Tatars   21, 25
Tatarstan   26, 43
Tsaritsyn   11, 21
UNESCO   41-42, 43
Valdai Hills   13
Volga-Baltic Waterway   15
"Volga Boatman"   27
Volga Day   43
Volga-Don Canal   16
Volga German Autonomous Soviet
    Socialist Republic   23
Volga Germans   22-23
Volga River
    Battle of Stalingrad and   5-10
    length of   13
    path of   13-14
    elevation of   14
    delta   14, 30, 32-33
    tributaries of   14
    canals and   15, 21, 37
    history of   19-26
    industry and   23, 38-40
    dams and   23-24, 37-38
    shipping and   24
    plant life and   29-31
    animal life and   29, 31-33
    pollution and   35, 40-42, 43
Volga River system   14
Volgograd Bridge   17
Volgograd   11, 14, 17, 21, 38, 43
Volgoverkhovye   13, 14
Von Paulus, General Friedrich   9
World War II   5
Yeltsin, Boris   41

ABOUT THE AUTHOR

Joanne Mattern is the author of more than 200 nonfiction books for young readers. Her books for Mitchell Lane include biographies of notables such as Michelle Obama, Count Basie, Benny Goodman, Blake Lively, Selena, Lebron James, and Peyton Manning. She especially enjoys traveling and exploring new places. Joanne lives in New York State with her husband, four children, and an assortment of pets.